Unsolved Mysteries

C O N T E N T S

Collins *Children's Books*

Beasts from the Deep

We actually know very little about life on the sea bed or at the bottom of lakes. There are unfathomable depths that no one has ever reached, even with modern diving equipment.

Nessie, the loch monster

Loch Ness in Scotland is 250m deep. The water is so cold that nothing lives in the water below 40m. Or does it? There have been many reported sightings of Nessie but there is no proof of her existence.

Some scientists think Nessie could be the last dinosaur – which would make her 65 million years old.

Mystery snapshot

The most famous picture of Nessie was taken in 1934 by R.K. Wilson – do you think it is real? Naturalists say it is actually a photograph of an otter or bird because the ripples in the water are huge in comparison to the size of the animal's 'head'.

NESSIE – FACT OR FICTION?

Let's play Nessie guessie

A family likeness?

Different people who have spotted Nessie seem to describe different monsters. Is there more than one Nessie? Could there be a whole family of Nessies?

Monster-spotting

1 The long-necked monster has been sighted all over the world. It swims through the water at amazing speeds and bounds along on land like a sea-lion.

2 The merhorse has been spotted on at least 37 occasions. It is believed to be about 30m long and lives on a diet of squid.

3 The many-humped monster is thought to live in the warmer parts of the Atlantic Ocean. It swims with a caterpillar-like movement.

4 The super-otter is reputed to be over 20m long and has webbed feet.

Make-believe mermaid

In 1822, Captain Eades exhibited a dead mermaid in London. Thousands of people paid to see this creature which was later found to be made of half an ape and half a giant fish sewn together!

ANCIENT FISH

A coelacanth fish that was thought to be extinct for 65 million years was caught off the South African coast on 22 December 1938. During the late 1980s several coelacanths were seen living 200m below the surface in the Indian Ocean.

Monster Footprints

Around the world and over the centuries there have been many tales of sightings of mysterious ape-like creatures, much larger than humans. Here's your chance to meet some of them!

The Abominable Snowman

The Abominable Snowman is believed to inhabit the world's highest mountain range, the Himalayas. In 1970 two climbers, Dougal Haston and Don Whillan, encountered a set of inexplicably huge footprints. Later, in the moonlight, Haston spotted an ape-like creature bounding across the slopes.

... or Yeti

The locals accept the existence of the Abominable Snowman but they have called it the Yeti, which means 'dweller among the rocks'. However, no one has proved that there is a Yeti.

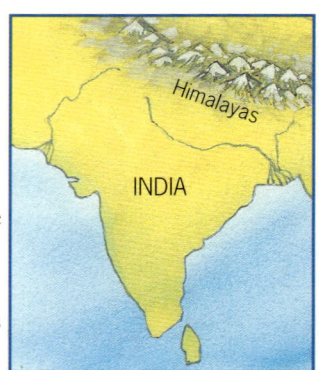

MYSTERY MUG SHOT

This creature was killed by François de Loys in 1917 on the border between Venezuela and Colombia, in South America. Is it a hominid (early human being) or an ape? It is certainly not an animal that can be identified by scientists.

So you don't believe in monsters?

WHO'S PULLING YOUR LEG?

According to local folklore, the Orang Pendek inhabits the forests of Sumatra. This monster is supposed to be able to talk in its own language and have feet that face backwards. Mummified Orang Pendeks were sold to tourists. But as long ago as the 13th century, the traveller Marco Polo saw these mummies being made from the corpses of lemurs and other monkeys!

Bigfoot on film?

It's not hard to see how Bigfoot got its name! It is also known by its Native American name, Sasquatch. Estimates of Bigfoot's height vary, but it could be between two and three metres. This picture is a still from a film shot in Northern California by Roger Paltram in 1967. It looks slightly human, leading some people to believe it is a hoax.

What a whopper

This huge plastercast caused a sensation in 1958. It was made by a truck driver from massive footprints near his cabin in California. In 1969, in Washington State, a continuous trail of over 1,000 footprints was found, stretching for more than one kilometre.

Puzzling Pyramids

About 80 pyramids were built in Ancient Egypt between 3100 and 320BC as burial sites for their pharaohs. How were these amazing structures built?

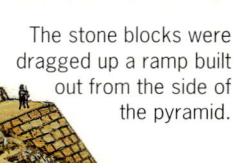

It probably took 100,000 workers and 30 years to build the Great Pyramid.

The stone blocks were dragged up a ramp built out from the side of the pyramid.

The pharaoh would choose the site for his own pyramid many years before he expected to die.

PYRAMID STATISTICS

• The Great Pyramid is made out of 2,300,000 separate blocks of stone.
• Each block weighs an average of 2.5 tonnes.
• At 137.5m, the Great Pyramid is three times the height of the Statue of Liberty.

Unanswered questions
How did the Egyptians cut the stone so precisely? No tool has been found which would have been strong enough to cut stone into accurate blocks.

Could the Egyptians have built ships huge enough and stable enough to transport the stone down the River Nile from their quarry at Tura to the pyramid building site at Giza?

ORION

Spirits in the stars

The pyramids may have been used as observatories. The position of the pyramids at Giza matches exactly the position of the stars in the constellation of Orion. Historians think that shafts like this one (left), cut into the walls of the pyramids, were used as astronomical viewing chambers. Perhaps the ancient Egyptians believed that the spirits of their dead pharaohs would live forever among the stars.

Farewell to a pharaoh

The bodies of the dead pharaohs were bound in strips of resin-soaked linen to preserve them. The mummified corpse was then placed in an elaborately decorated coffin before being entombed in the pyramid.

VIEWING SHAFT

COFFIN MADE FROM HOLLOWED OUT LOGS

OTHER PYRAMIDS

YUCATAN PYRAMID

The Aztec, Inca and Mayan civilisations of South America also constructed huge pyramids from stone or sun-baked mud bricks. Often, the pyramids were built high up in the mountains. How did the builders drag the huge stones without the invention of the wheel?

The Mayan people did not have metal tools, so how did they carve the huge stone blocks for their pyramids?

CHICHEN ITZA

Flying Saucers

People have seen Unidentified Flying Objects for hundreds of years, but, until recently, no one took these sightings seriously. After space travel became possible in the 1960s, people became more willing to accept the possibility of life forms visiting us from other planets.

A name that stuck

On 24 June 1947, Kenneth Arnold was flying his small plane over Washington State when he saw nine 'saucer-like things' flying ahead of him. Arnold's description of these mysterious objects stuck and we have been calling UFOs 'flying saucers' ever since.

PARK YOUR SPACECRAFT HERE!

The population of Elmwood, Wisconsin, USA saw so many UFOs during the 1980s that they voted to build a landing strip in a field. They decided to decorate the field with a picture of an alien shaking hands with a human.

The Rosewell incident

The people of Rosewell, New Mexico saw a massive disc-shaped thing flying over their town on 2 July 1947. The next day, a ranch owner found a wrecked object scattered all over his land. Major Jesse Marcel from a nearby army base collected the wreckage but it was then taken away by the US government and was never shown to the public. Was it the remains of a UFO?

KIDNAPPED BY ALIENS

Charles Hickson and Calvin Parker say that they were kidnapped by grey aliens with claw-like hands, wrinkled skin and slit eyes while they were fishing in Mississippi on the night of 11 October 1973.

It was a dark night but as they sat in their fishing boat, Hickson and Parker saw a strange object hovering over the water in front of them.

Then three creatures floated out of the UFO and moved towards the two men. The aliens carried Hickson and Parker into their spaceship.

Hickson and Parker found themselves in a brightly lit room. They were examined by the aliens and then taken back to their fishing boat.

UFOs from long ago

Some Chinese etchings dating back 50,000 years are thought to be the oldest pictures we have of alien spaceships. The drawings are of cigar-shaped UFOs.

Calling all aliens

This plate is fixed to the Pioneer 10 space probe. It gives directions for finding Earth and shows what humans are like. One day it may be found by aliens.

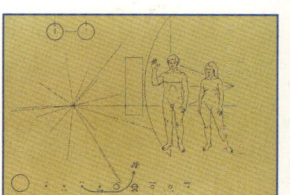

The Baffling Bermuda Triangle

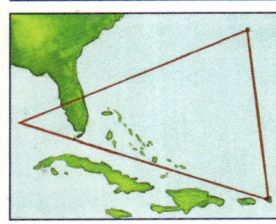

The Bermuda Triangle lies in the Western Atlantic, off the coast of Florida. No one has been able to explain why so many planes and ships have been lost without trace in this stretch of ocean.

The fate of Flight 19

At 3.45pm the leader of Flight 19, Lieutenant Charles Taylor, called into flight control hysterically repeating that he was lost.

At 4.30pm Lieutenant Harry Cone took off from Banana River naval station with a rescue team of 12 men in his Martin Mariner flying boat. This huge plane reported back to flight control twice and then disappeared without trace.

Just after 7pm Flight 19 sent their final message – 'FT . . . FT'. This was part of their call sign. Then there was nothing. Six planes with a crew of 27 had just disappeared into thin air.

Five Avenger torpedo bomber planes made up Flight 19 on 5 December 1945.

Futile search

Even though hundreds of aircraft and 20 ships searched 480,000 square kilometres of ocean over the next few weeks, no wreckage or bodies were ever found.

VANISHING SHIPS

Between 1840 and 1984 no less than 20 ships have disappeared in the Bermuda Triangle. Most of them sank without trace and the wrecks have never been discovered. A few lost radio contact and were then found drifting in the Atlantic without their crews.

The Marine Sulphur Queen *vanished in 1963 along with all its crew.*

Imaginary islands?

In June 1974, pilot Carolyn Cascio was flying from Nassau to Grand Turk Island in the Bahamas. As she flew over Grand Turk the islanders saw her but she couldn't see them. She radioed a nearby airport, telling them that she could see two uninhabited islands. Contact was then lost and her plane vanished.

A plane lost in time?

A National Airline plane disappeared from air traffic control radar as it approached Miami airport. Ten minutes later it reappeared. None of the passengers had noticed anything unusual but, when the plane touched down on time, their watches were all 10 minutes slow.

THEORIES

• Are there weird magnetic forces that pull ships and planes into space?
• Is it just an area that experiences violent storms and hurricanes?
• Does methane gas from the sea bed sink ships and bring down planes?
• Or is it the gateway to another dimension?

Lost at Sea

Did you know that the sailors who manned the galleons in the 15th and 16th centuries never learned to swim? Sailors were very superstitious and suspected that monsters roamed the sea. They didn't learn to swim because they wanted to drown before anything else got to them...

The story of the *Mary Celeste*

On 5 November 1892 Captain Benjamin Briggs steered the *Mary Celeste* out of New York harbour, heading for Italy with his wife and baby daughter, a crew of seven and a cargo of wine. They disappeared after leaving the harbour.

On 5 December the *Mary Celeste* was spotted and a boarding party was sent to the ship. There was no one on board. The last entry in the ship's log had been on 24 November.

The shape of the Captain's daughter could still be seen in her unmade bed; breakfast had been left half eaten; a bottle of cough medicine stood open and unspilled, and on the cabin table, a slate was found with the words...

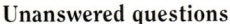

'Fanny my dear wife. Frances MR.'

Unanswered questions

Why did the crew abandon ship? What happened to them? Were they eaten by sharks? Were they captured by pirates? Did Captain Briggs go mad? Why were their bodies never found?

12

Phantoms afloat

A 17th-century ghost ship called *The Flying Dutchman* has haunted sailors for centuries. Captain Cornelius Vanderdecken, was condemned to wander the oceans for all time in his doomed vessel.

THE FLYING DUTCHMAN

GEORGE V

Royal rendezvous

The future King George V and 12 other men on his ship *HMS Inconstant* saw *The Flying Dutchman* on 11 July 1881, while they were sailing around Australia.

U-boat U-turn

Rear Admiral Donitz, Hitler's top sea commander, reported that one of his fearless U-Boat crews refused to go on another tour of duty to Suez because they had seen *The Flying Dutchman*.

Seaside spectre

In 1939, 100 swimmers relaxing at False Bay on the South African coast saw *The Flying Dutchman*.

A CHRISTMAS MYSTERY

Today, a deserted lighthouse stands on a large rock in the Outer Hebrides. But once it was operated by three men. When a steamship called on 26 December 1900 to deliver supplies, it found the lighthouse locked and empty. The men had disappeared into thin air leaving everything in order and their beds made. Their bodies were never found.

13

Vanishing Acts

What happens to people who simply disappear? Do they take up a new identity and start a new life somewhere else or are they taken against their will?

Amelia Earhart

The famous pilot Amelia Earhart and her navigator, Fred Noonan, disappeared without a trace on 3 July 1937. Her plane was never found and neither of the aviators were ever seen again.

Amelia and Fred were last seen setting off from Puerto Rico.

What happened to Amelia?

Did Fred Noonan get lost? With no land in sight and no fuel left did they ditch into the sea? If this is what happened then why did the huge search operation that followed fail to find them?

Secret spies?

Were Amelia and Fred really on a secret mission? Had they been told to fly over the Japanese-held Mariana Islands to photograph military bases? Was the plane shot down and the pilots executed by the Japanese?

Tunnel trick

In the winter of 1975 Mr and Mrs Jackson Wright were driving to New York in a blizzard.

When they reached the Lincoln Tunnel they agreed to stop the car so that they could clear the snow from the windscreens. That was the last Mr Wright, or anyone else, ever saw of his wife, Martha.

The ghost legion?

The Ninth Legion of the Roman Empire was stationed at York during the first century AD. Suddenly, the legion disappeared from all Roman records and its barracks were deserted. What happened to the legion? Was it totally destroyed by rebels?

APPEARING PEOPLE

• A young man called Kaspar Hauser turned up in Nuremberg in 1828 with no idea of where he had come from or who he was... Unfortunately Kaspar was then murdered in 1883.

• In Germany in 1851 a man called Joseph Vorin insisted that he came from the city of Laxaria in the country of Sakria – both non-existent places.

• In Paris in 1905 a man was found speaking a language which no one has been able to identify. Eventually he found a way to communicate and claimed that he came from a city called Lisbian – which again, doesn't exist.

KASPAR HAUSER

15

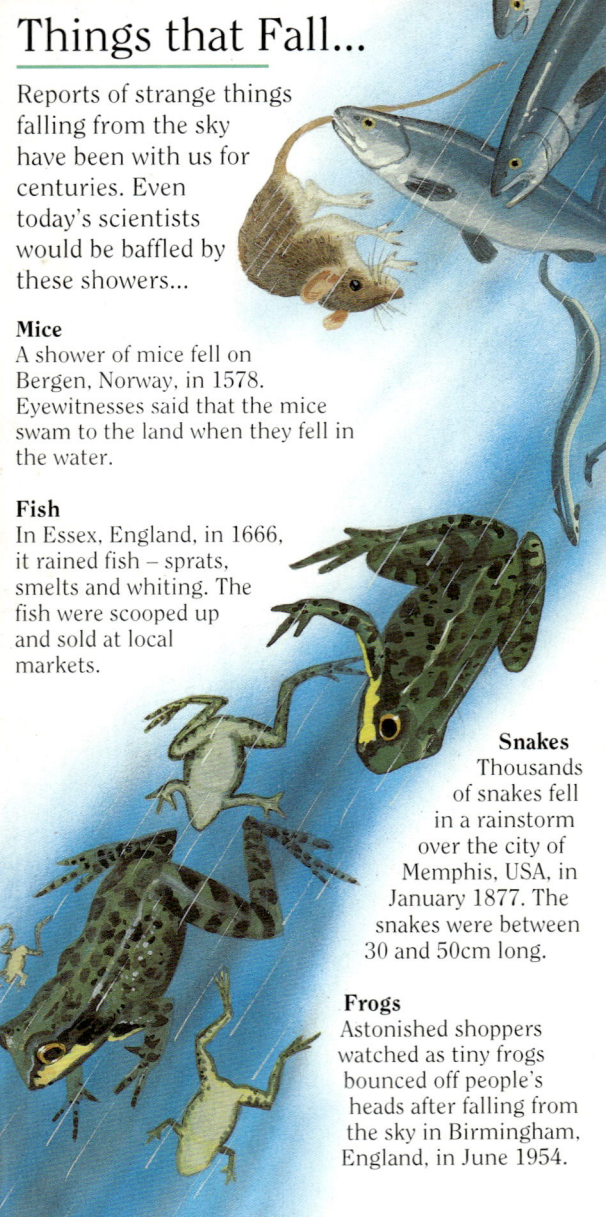

Things that Fall...

Reports of strange things falling from the sky have been with us for centuries. Even today's scientists would be baffled by these showers...

Mice
A shower of mice fell on Bergen, Norway, in 1578. Eyewitnesses said that the mice swam to the land when they fell in the water.

Fish
In Essex, England, in 1666, it rained fish – sprats, smelts and whiting. The fish were scooped up and sold at local markets.

Snakes
Thousands of snakes fell in a rainstorm over the city of Memphis, USA, in January 1877. The snakes were between 30 and 50cm long.

Frogs
Astonished shoppers watched as tiny frogs bounced off people's heads after falling from the sky in Birmingham, England, in June 1954.

...From the Sky

Killer plate

On 9 November 1950, a farm in Devon was struck by ice-meteors as large as plates – one of them was so enormous that it chopped the head off an unlucky sheep!

Damage left by the ice bomb.

Monster hailstones

A couple on holiday in France in August 1981 were caught in a hailstorm on a beautiful sunny day. The hailstones were big enough to smash the windscreen and dent the car doors.

Exploding ceiling!

Mrs Fox's two children were playing in their bedroom early in the morning on 28 September 1980 when the ceiling exploded, showering ice and debris over the room. The biggest chunk of ice ended up embedded in the floor, only just avoiding the children.

PENNIES FROM HEAVEN

On 28 May 1982, pennies dropped from the sky and landed in the graveyard of St Elizabeth's Church in Reddish. The coins fell on their edges and were stuck in the earth. The surprised vicar of St Elizabeth's tried throwing coins to see if they usually landed on their edges. He found it impossible to make the money land in this way. Why don't you have a go... can you manage it?

17

Supernatural Stones

All over the world there are unexplained monuments left by ancient peoples. In Europe there are thousands of weird stone circles. On Easter Island in the Pacific eerie stone figures haunt the landscape.

Stonehenge

People began building Stonehenge on Salisbury Plain at about the same time as the ancient Egyptians started using hieroglyphics. But unlike the Egyptians, the builders of Stonehenge had not developed a system of writing so there are no inscriptions to give us any clues about this mysterious monument.

What was it for?

No one knows. People have suggested that Stonehenge was a memorial to dead kings, a castle, a graveyard, a calendar, a horoscope, a druid temple, a computer, an observatory or a hospital. What do you think it was for?

Who built it?

We know that each of the four-tonne stones of Stonehenge was transported 300km from Wales, starting in about 3000BC – but we don't know who moved the stones or how they did it.

MERLIN

According to legend, Stonehenge was flown through the air from Ireland by Merlin the wizard, at the time of King Arthur.

Easter Island aliens?

Hundreds of huge sculptures stand all over Easter Island, in the Pacifc Ocean. Back in AD1100, how did the primitive islanders carve such hard volcanic rock with simple tools? The people of Easter Island do not look anything like the statues. Could the sculptures be portraits of visitors from another planet?

HOW THEY DID IT

The statues were carved from rocky outcrops high up in the mountains.

A rope was tied round the statue and it was rolled downhill on tree trunks.

At the bottom of the track they dug a deep pit into which the statue was lowered.

The stones of Carnac

Nearly 3,000 colossal standing stones were erected at Carnac in Brittany, north-western France, around 2000BC. They are arranged in parallel rows, some stretching for over 1km. We have no idea who constructed this impressive monument.

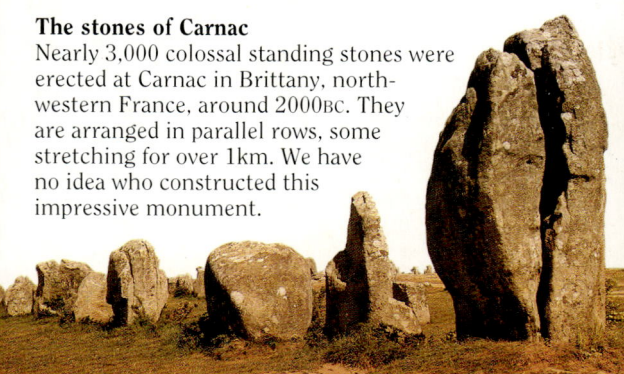

Lines, Circles and Pictures

In ancient times people drew strange pictures in the landscape. There are spiders in South America and horses in southern England. What do these pictures mean and why were they drawn?

Ancient lines

In 1927 a surveyor flew above the remote Nazca desert in Peru to plan a new road. He saw huge pictures cut into the ground below. They were drawn by the Nazca Native Americans around 200BC. As well as pictures of animals, there are also 13,000 absolutely straight lines etched into the rock. Some of them are more than 32km long. The only way the Nazca Lines can be understood is from the air – so how did the Nazca Native Americans draw pictures they wouldn't be able to see?

High-flyers?

A theory has been put forward that the Nazcan people *could* fly. Evidence shows that they had the technology to put together a hot-air balloon.

...or just a lot of hot air?

So the Nazcans may have been able to organise the drawing up of the lines and figures from the air. But the theory has yet to be proved.

Other theories

Some people think the lines are landing directions for spacecraft. Others believe they are maps of the stars, used by the Nazcan people to tell them when to plant and harvest their crops.

Circles from space?

Between 1980 and 1991 strange shapes suddenly began appearing in farmers' fields in the south of England. Huge, perfectly shaped circles were etched into cornfields overnight – at first no one knew how they were made or who created them. Crop circles are now known to be elaborate hoaxes, but there are still those who dismiss the logical explanation and believe that the circles were made by aliens trying to get in touch with us.

It's a lot less bovver with a hover!

CROP CIRCLE

HORSE BOX

The White Horse at Uffington in Oxfordshire measures 114 metres across and, like other carvings, can be seen from many miles around.

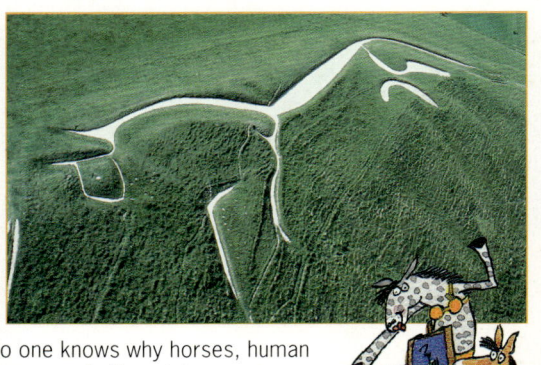

No one knows why horses, human figures and other pictures were carved on chalk hillsides in southern England during Iron Age times. Were they tribal symbols to warn off rival tribes? Were they fertility idols, worshipped to bring good harvests?

21

Spooky Stories

Poltergeist means 'noisy ghost'. Being invisible, poltergeists often cause a lot of disturbance which has sometimes been caught on film. Ghosts are shadowy silent figures and no one has ever been able to prove that they exist.

THE HAUNTED HOUSE

On 31 August 1977 the most famous poltergeist in Britain began haunting the Harper family home in Enfield, London.

Over the next 14 months witnesses reported over 400 'happenings'. Money was burnt, marbles rushed across the floor, sofas somersaulted over backwards and teapots danced across the kitchen.

A photographer from the *Daily Mirror* set up cameras to record anything he could. He managed to capture the poltergeist whipping the blankets off one of the children's beds.

BENT GAS PIPE

THESE MATCHBOXES BURNT BUT THE MATCHES DIDN'T!

SIGNS OF A POLTERGEIST

Knocking and scraping sounds
Footsteps
Disappearing objects
Flying furniture
Scribbling on walls

The pub poltergeist
In November 1900 a poltergeist hunter travelled to a public house in Via Bava in Turin, Italy, to investigate a haunting. When he went down to the wine cellar six bottles floated off the shelf and fell to the floor.

The ghost hitch-hiker

In 1970 a motorcycle policeman. Mahmood Ali of Peshwar, India, gave a lift to a young woman dressed in white. Before the journey was over the girl had disappeared from the back of his bike. Mahmood later discovered that a young woman had been killed in a car crash at the point where he had picked up the girl.

Double trouble

A French teacher, Emilie Sagée, once saw her 'doppelgänger' or ghostly double as she walked past her classroom window. Her terrified pupils also saw two teachers: one inside and one outside. As a result, poor Miss Sagée was sacked by the school.

A ROYAL GHOST

The ghost of Henry VIII's third wife, Lady Catherine Howard, haunts Hampton Court Palace every year on the anniversary of the night she was arrested by Henry's soldiers in 1541.

The 19-year-old queen broke away and ran screaming and crying down a corridor – now known as the Haunted Gallery. She knew she was going to be beheaded.

HAMPTON COURT PALACE

People who Float, Hypnotise...

Most of us go through life with our feet firmly on the ground, but there are some people who float through the air, go off into a hypnotic trance or even explode.

An uplifting experience

In 1852 Daniel Douglas Home lifted himself off the floor and placed his hands on the ceiling for the first time. He continued to levitate for the next 40 years – often in front of hundreds of people. Even the Emperor Napoleon III saw Home levitate.

Flying saints

Hundreds of Catholic saints have been credited with the power of levitation. St Joseph of Copertino was so happy when he levitated that he often offered to carry people's things for them!

Money for old rope?

Is this Indian fakir's assistant really suspended above a length of rope in the air? The Indian rope trick has been performed for centuries and travellers to India paid huge sums to watch this gravity-defying feat. What you can't see in this old photograph is that the boy is in fact balancing on thin taught wires. For obvious reasons, the trick was usually performed at dusk!

Don't try this at home

People can do strange things when they are hypnotised. Believe it or not, the man in this picture went into a deep trance and became as stiff as a board.

Did you know?

In the USA the police sometimes hypnotise victims to help them remember vital evidence.

Hypnotic hangovers

Dr Prem Misra treats people in Scotland who are still suffering from hypnosis after volunteering at hypnotic shows. One of his patients is a man who can't stop himself taking all his clothes off every time he hears a hand clap!

... and Explode

The case of the exploding doctor

On 5 December 1966, postman Don Gosnell called in on Dr John Bentley of 403 Main Street, Coudersport, Pennsylvania. Instead of the 92-year-old man, he discovered a light blue smoke hovering in the air, a pile of ash on the floor of the bathroom and half a leg. That was all that remained of Dr Bentley... he had just burst into flames.

How does it happen?

Some scientists have shown that spontaneous combustion coincides with magnetic surges through the Earth, but no one knows if there is a definite connection.

Mysterious People

Do some people have special powers that enable them to talk to ghosts, know what other people are thinking, or exercise mind over matter?

Supernatural know-how

In 1974 a priceless painting was stolen from Kenwood House in north London. A psychic detective called Nella realised that she knew about the robbery and got in touch with the police. After the police had ruled her out as a suspect, they invited Nella to help with the investigation.

THE STOLEN VERMEER PAINTING

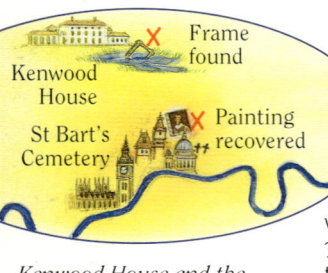

Kenwood House and the cemetery where the picture was eventually found.

Three steps to success

1 Nella's strange powers meant she knew where the picture frame had been dumped.
2 She accurately predicted that the police would receive ransom notes.
3 Finally she told the police they would find the painting in a London cemetery and, a few days later, they did.

DALAI LAMA

Life after death?

Tibetans believe that their spiritual leader, the Dalai Lama, is the reincarnation of a previous Dalai Lama whose soul enters the body of a child born at the exact moment of his death. But before the child is accepted as the new Dalai Lama he must correctly answer questions about his former life as proof of his reincarnation.

Can dreams come true?

For Chris Robinson the answer is yes. In July 1993 he dreamt about colliding jet aircraft. He even drew these pictures of the escape parachutes. The next day he saw a promotion for an airshow, so he rushed off to the airfield and tried to warn officials of the impending danger, just minutes before two MiG jet fighters collided in mid air. Miraculously the pilots survived... thanks to their emergency parachutes.

One of the fighter planes in flames.

Play it again, Rosemary

In 1964 Rosemary Brown bought a piano. She then found herself being visited by the ghosts of great composers, who came to her to dictate unfinished works. In 1966 Beethoven dictated his Tenth Symphony.

ROUND THE BEND?

Uri Geller went on British television in 1973 and by sheer concentration managed to bend spoons, forks and keys. Cutlery lying on the studio table bent without him even touching it. Geller convinced many people that he possessed remarkable powers of Extra Sensory Perception, but others think he is nothing more than a con-man.

GELLER AND ONE OF HIS FAMOUS SPOONS

27

Is the future written in the stars? For hundreds of years astrologers have used the movements of the stars to make predictions. Do you agree with them in believing that the stars control our destiny?

THE ZODIAC

The signs of the zodiac are the names of groups of stars or constellations. Do you think you are a typical example of your star sign?

Nostradamus – the world's most famous astrologer.

Aries
22 Mar – 20 Apr
Fiery, impulsive.

Taurus
21 Apr – 21 May
Patient, affectionate.

Gemini
22 May – 22 Jun
Sensitive, artistic.

Cancer
23 Jun – 23 Jul
Caring, emotional.

Leo
24 Jul – 23 Aug
Dramatic, loyal.

Virgo
24 Aug – 23 Sept
Reliable, perfectionist.

Libra
24 Sept – 23 Oct
Fair, positive.

Scorpio
24 Oct – 22 Nov
Witty, passionate.

Sagittarius
23 Nov – 22 Dec
Determined, energetic.

Capricorn
23 Dec – 19 Jan
Steady, logical.

Aquarius
20 Jan – 19 Feb
Original, independent.

Pisces
20 Feb – 21 Mar
Calm, dreamy.

THE CHINESE HOROSCOPE

Chinese astrology is thousands of years old. It is based on a 12 year cycle started by Emperor Huang Ti in 2637BC. A different animal is assigned to each of the 12 years. So in Chinese astrology the year you were born in is more important than the time of year.

Rat
1972, 1984, 1996
Cool, charming.

Horse
1966, 1978, 1990
Cheerful, popular.

Ox
1961, 1973, 1985
Quiet, easygoing.

Sheep
1967, 1979, 1991
Creative, gentle.

Tiger
1962, 1974, 1986
Powerful, born leaders!

Monkey
1968, 1980, 1992
Successful, talkative.

Rabbit
1963, 1975, 1987
Gifted, ambitious.

Rooster / Chicken
1969, 1981, 1993
Thoughtful, eccentric.

Dragon
1964, 1976, 1988
Honest, stubborn.

Dog
1970, 1982, 1994
Loyal, hard-working.

Snake
1965, 1977, 1989
Wise, determined.

Pig/ Boar
1971, 1983, 1995
Kind, shy.

All in the Mind?

Some people use the stars to reveal their destiny. Others use anything from bumps on their head to a pack of cards to discover more about themselves.

A guide to your palm

People have been reading palms for over 7,000 years. But can lines on your palms really have anything to do with your personality or your future?

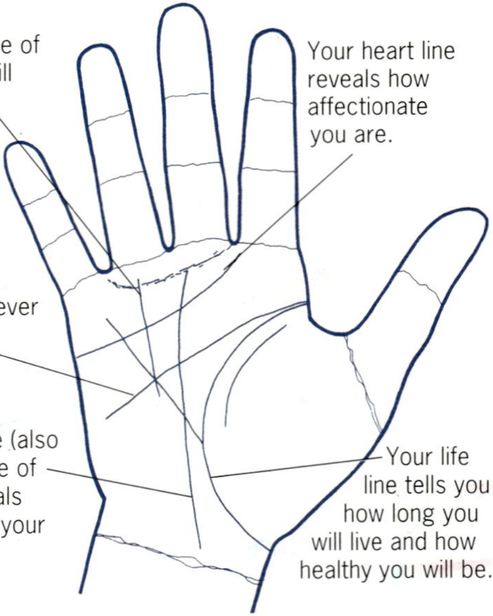

If you have a prominent line of Apollo you will be very successful.

Your heart line reveals how affectionate you are.

How long is your head line? It's supposed to show how clever you are.

Your fate line (also called the line of Saturn) reveals how fulfilling your life will be.

Your life line tells you how long you will live and how healthy you will be.

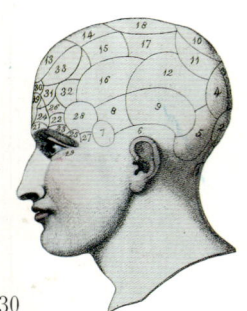

Barmy bumps

In the 19th century phrenology was quite a craze. Phrenologists believed that you could tell what someone's personality was like by feeling the bumps on their skulls. Why don't you try it with a friend!

Oh no — I've hit a low!

Biorhythm blues

Some people think that from the day you are born, your body follows three cycles which affect your physical, mental and intellectual health.

Some companies take biorhythms very seriously. Japanese bus operators ban drivers from working when all three cycles hit a low point in an attempt to avoid crashes.

TAROT

Tarot cards are used by fortune-tellers. The cards you choose from the pack are supposed to reveal information about your personality and your future.

Wheel of fortune

This strange looking object is actually a special Chinese compass. According to the laws of geomancy, the position of your house or even where you put the furniture in your bedroom will affect the harmony and happiness in your life. Believe it or not, some large companies in the USA have used the geomancy compass to decide the layout of their offices. Managers hope that the resulting design will help to motivate their staff.

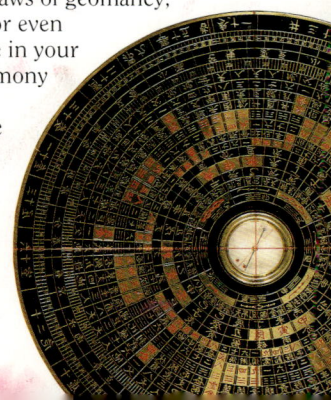

INDEX

First published in 1996 by HarperCollins
Children's Books,
A Division of HarperCollins Publishers Ltd,
77-85 Fulham Palace Road,
London W6 8JB
ISBN: 0 00 197918 3

Illustrations: Charlotte Hard and
Tony Smith

Photographs: Ancient Art and Architecture
Collection 7l; Ann Ronan at Image Select 28,
30; Ann Ronan Picture Library 25t; English
Heritage Photographic Library 26t; Fortean
Picture Library 2, 4, 24t, /Patterson/Gimlin/ ©
1968 René Dahinden 3t, /René Dahinden 3c,
/Stephen C. Pratt 8, /Dennis Stacy 9, /©
1976/1993 Larry E. Arnold 25b; Frank Spooner
Pictures 27t, /Gamma 26b; Hulton Deutsch
14t, 14b; Image Select 13; Images Colour
Library 19t, 20, 27b; Images/Charles Walker

Collection 15, 21t, 21b, 29, 31; Mary Evans
Picture Library/Lawrie Berger 22t, /Guy Lyon
Playfair 22cl, 22cr /Harry Price College,
University of London 24b; Planet Earth
Pictures/Peter Scoones 5; Rex Features 27c;
Science Photo Library/John Meade 18;
Spectrum Colour Library 7r; Zefa 6, /Damm 23.

A CIP record for this book is available
from the British Library

Printed and bound in Hong Kong